A Young Woman Evolving the Vision of the Future

A Young Woman Evolving *the* Vision *of the* Future

THE FUTURE NEEDS YOU

THEKGO NGWANAKGAU NKADIMENG

PARTRIDGE
A Penguin Random House Company

To order additional copies of this book, contact
Toll Free 0800 990 914 (South Africa)
+44 20 3014 3997 (outside South Africa)
orders.africa@partridgepublishing.com

www.partridgepublishing.com/africa

CONTENTS

DEDICATIONS

I wrote this book trying to tell a story of the little I have observed in this world, realizing what being a woman is and what some are lacking in this topic. And also emphasis on the topics we always avoid as people of this world. My hope was my voice to be heard by all nations

THIS BOOK IS DEDICATED TO

All women in the whole world with problems in accepting who they are and lacking confidence and love for themselves, I know one day you will get to realize that you are the best and beautiful. We are the strength of this world, and if you are the ones failing the world, it will fail too. Let's change this world together

All men to know how to look after women and make them special just the way they are. This world needs more men to know that any woman needs to be nurtured and protected no matter their status or looks. Real men start by respecting their moms; if they do then it will be easy to respect any female species they see

And all those teenage girls who want to know that they are special. If we can stick together we can change a lot of negativity. It is never about the looks and it was never about them, it is about self-love, self-acceptance and inner beauty

-Thekgo Nkadimeng

ACKNOWLEDGEMENTS

Writing this book required my mind, passion and enthusiasm. I would firstly like to thank my loving parents Mabodile and Abinkie Nkadimeng, the rocks and providers, whom brought me to this world and inspired me each and every day to be who I am and always loved me for me, I don't know how I can thank you for everything and the support you gave throughout my journey on this book.

And I would like to thank all this gifted men of God Dr David Molapo and Dr John C Maxwell with their inspiring books that they wrote, they really help me grow into a better person and believe in my writing skills.

Lastly without the Lord we are nothing, the one above makes me positive and to have faith in whatever situation I am facing and reminds that in his name everything is possible. As it all starts and ends with him. Giving me this vision and strength to write and letting my mind be heard by the world.

-Thekgo Nkadimeng

INTRODUCTION

You can be who you are,
With no doubt
BEING WOMEN

I know being a woman is very tough, not only having those labour pains and periods but in many ways like looking the best. You can ask yourself why but the answer is that we women we are so precious and we are moulded well by the Lord God with those breasts, curves and buttocks.

It is 21st century and things have become tougher and tougher for you as fashion, hairstyles, make up and accessories are being modernised and changed and even more beautiful, colourful and it's hard for us to choose, but my tip is that remember that not everything will look good on you cause we are all different.

You know the time I got in my teen years I started on realizing that being a woman is hard hey, cause I saw many changes on me physically, emotionally and mentally and the worst challenge was when I started recognising that I am starting to like boys and I was getting self-aggrandizing and trying in all means to look fine, the funniest part was when I was less than 13years old I never minded how I looked. And sometimes it got me thinking that WOW God knows what he's doing. When you start seeing your periods and looking at those hunkies, that's if you have unprotected sex you will be pregnant and get diseases in a younger age. Hard but fun hey?

And yeah friend I can tell you that our mothers are most important and playing a big role in our lives cause they know what we are going through, and how tough it is can be, but in most situation I so thank my dad that he had taste and married a woman like my mom as she is open and lets me learn from her. She explains everything to me and how being a good girl is hard especially these days and that this changes and feelings we have can get us into troubles and mistakes. Every day I pray and thank God that I was born from the womb of this lovely woman as she inspires me and give me strength, even though I never told her before but God knows.

LEARNING THE HARD WAY

To grow up we learn from the silly mistakes we did and the lessons we learned on the journey, no human being can say he or she is a pro when it comes to life because you never know what to expect in return, I sometimes tell friends that life is not like a test, you can't rate how it will be, but when taking a test you can rate yourself looking at the questions and what you studied. When you are a person, you have to be ready for anything cause life is a war, you can die, you can be crippled or you can lose the one you love tomorrow and that's why some say life screw us all, and again can say as a woman you must be ready for war if you are looking for love, you going to meet pastors, gangsters, perverts, etc. because when this people meet you they won't tell you who they really are, I mean it is something you have to always remind your mind, because for love you can be raped, killed or abused, it happens and this is reality. Women are so vulnerable in a way that even asking for a ride is dangerous, well we have a lot of predators.

In South Africa we are facing a biggest challenge whereby young women are facing teenage pregnancy and being infected by HIV/Aids, one night stands are still trending and new-born babies are still fatherless, being a single mom is seen as bravery and a real definition of a real woman.

Women suppression will always be there because they are stronger than men, I am saying this because I know how easily men can be pulled down and always striving to be at the top so that they can proof that they are warriors and strong. To emphasise my statement, I guess you all have seen that when a woman died first in a family you can all see the husband is a mess and stressed up, you find his clothes not clean and the children starting to become a burden to him, yes when the wife was still alive the man could be the lion that can threaten the kids to do the right things, because the wife was just standing there giving her man the power to prove to the kids who is the head, then when the wife dies he get to realise that the head without the neck is nothing. Women are born to cover the wrongs of their husbands, and if you think it's a big task then you not a woman.

It is really inspiring to see women taking charge of their lives, and working hard to reach their destiny, It hurts me when most man just don't get it that this people are extraordinary and without them the world is nothing. Real men don't beat up their women to prove who is the strongest, you must at least give your woman a chance to make you a better man, look at those single men out there, they may be the most rich but there is something lacking, they never get to feel the touch of a woman who will make them breakfast in bed, scrap their back and listen to their plans and stupid theories. "you never know what you had, until it is gone", that's what most men get to face because they didn't give their selves time to look beyond the beauty of their women, as they undermined them, They get to realise the good side when they are gone after many years of struggle. One thing that most women don't realise is that silence will never be the answer, at least try to make your man understand what you feel for the sake of your happiness, because men are stubborn sometimes but let me tell you something, their weakness is a you, if you can love them and be beside them all the way.

I know it is every girls dream to be a wife one day, what I can say from what I have observed in other marriages, you find the woman surrounded by a family but still lonely, because there is a third party outside the relationship, it is not recommended but it happens. Sometimes it's our problem because we get to stop taking care of ourselves after wearing the rock on the finger, but sometimes men can be greedy, what I can say is that there are many alluring women out there but you can't have them all. Love your partner for what s/he is.

YOU ARE SPECIAL WOMEN

As I said that the lord made you extraordinary and strong than man, please read this piece I got on the net and maybe it will help you to keep on going forward because whatever challenge you are facing the lord is with you.

Why are you crying?, a young boy asked his mom. "Because I am a woman, she told him.

"I don't understand," he said.

His mom just hugged him and said, "And you never will, but that's okay."…

Later the little boy asked his father, "Why does mom seem to cry for no reason?"

"All women cry for no reason." Was all the man could say? The little boy grew up and became a man, still wondering why women cry. Finally he put in a call to God and when God got back to him he asked "God, why do women cry so easily?"

God answered "when I made a woman, I decided she had to be special. I made her shoulders strong enough to carry the weight of the world, yet, made her arms gentle enough to give comfort... I gave her the inner strength to endure childbirth and the rejection that many times will come even from her own children. I gave her a hardness that allow her to keep going and take care of her family and friends, even when everyone else give up, through sickness and fatigue without complaining... I gave her the sensitivity to love her children under any and all circumstances. Even when her child has hurt her badly... she has a very special power to make a child's boo-boo feel better and quell a teenager's anxieties and fears... I gave her strength to care for her husband, despite faults and I fashioned her from his rib to protect his heart... I gave her wisdom to know that a good husband never hurts his wife, but sometimes tests her strength and her resolve to stand beside him unfalteringly... for all of this hard work, I also gave her a tear to shed. It is hers to use whenever needed and! It is her only weakness... when you see her cry, tell her how much you love her, and all she does for everyone, and even though she may cry, you will have made her heart feel special!

This is a reminder for all men to understand why women are so wonderful.

CHAPTER 1

OUR CONFIDENCE

Don't you ask yourself why your father is always waiting for your mom to finish up when they are going somewhere in public? Well it is easy we are always the ones to finish last because we always want to look the best and that's in our nature, it simply shows loving who we are and confident.

Again ask yourself why you always put make up and do those Brazilian hair, I can tell you that your face only can give a good impression and you know that is what men check before they even think of asking you out.

Every time I look into my mirror, truly speaking I look at myself with all my attention from head to toe because obviously I have to be confident and walk tall when I am at town or at the mall and feel like I own this world. No human is defined ugly or unlikable to me it's a big no,

I remember one time I logged on Facebook and found a status written by a guy who is one of my friends he wrote "if you want to see how ugly your girl is, just let her wash her face and sleep then in the morning you will see what I am talking about" it firstly got me angry but when time went on I noticed that nature is important, we women hide ourselves too much to an extend that the person living with you don't really know your REAL looks but with men it is bald head and they put no makeup like we do and they are so natural, that is why they mock us. But I don't blame you just don't overdo it.

THE PERSON IN YOU

There is something I hate about us women, we tend to change who we are and get so unreal in our daily lives because we don't have love and confidence in ourselves. Ask me why, because it sometimes happens to me, feeling down or feeling like a loser.

"None of us was born confident. Health self-esteem is crucial to boost your confidence. Although you cannot change your past, the right decisions and action you take today will shape your future. We therefore need to work at developing our healthy self-image. I must emphasise that a healthy self-image doesn't imply pride or arrogance." – Dr David Molapo

This part I wrote here made me realise that no one can change the negativity I have in me but myself. So think if you didn't think about it then it is time for you to do self-analysis and realise were you stand. Because I think it's time we take a positive look at ourselves. I know those weaves and make up hide our scares and every bad thing you think should be hidden but always know that what is outside you is nothing compared to the inner you, your heart knows it all, those looks are just a shell to keep that heart safe.

I always read magazines were I get to find an article written about women saying they never loved their selves. As they feels everyone looks down at them due to different reasons. And in one other magazine I read there was a part were Relebogile Mabotja had to say her part, as we all know she has an African body. She said "I think everyone in general- skinny, fat, straight, gay, men, women, and lesbians need to love themselves. So I am going through a period of putting myself first and paying more attention of taking a better care of myself. I am learning to say no and spending more time with myself so that I can know myself more".

So that got me thinking whether you like it or not people will never get out of comments, so what you have to do is love yourself more. Most of the time women are changed from what they are because of what people say, it all start like" you have a big body, you have to lose weight", then you lose it, after that they say" you look great but your nose is so big, it looks more big when you lost weight", I know some are familiar with this kind of stories and did what people want until they were out of options. You will never satisfy all those comments and truly speaking they can take you down slowly, they are like silent killers because you will never do what other people want you to do and get it alright until you end up trying to commit suicide. Put in mind that words are so powerful they can take you down and kill you slowly that is why we avoid emotional abuses.

I have learned that you have to love yourself before others do because that will always help you in being realistic and stop imitating other people, I am saying this because I know many women change who they are to impress the next person, some out there wear clothes which they are not comfortable with, they become somebody they are not and they change their characters to impress other people, they become dependent to someone and can't even say no even if they know it is so wrong and most of the time its men who do that, comparing us with the next person as if they don't know variation is there so we will never be the same. Now my friend its time you put those people in their positions that you not some trash cause your mother kept you for nine months just like any other human being. And a tip ladies know if someone says you are not hot just say" of cause I am not your typical hotty", cause men can stress you and drive you to be someone else.

<u>LEARN TO BE WHO YOU ARE AND BE PROUD!</u>

Guess you now know that the person in you is more important than the outer shell, meaning that beauty can change anytime due to many reasons but your character will never change and that is what makes you what you are and the reason why people treat you the way they do at the moment so you better be proud of you cause that define you.

<u>LET'S LOOK AT A GREATER LOOK OF DEFINE:</u>

DESTINY- destiny is the future destined for a person or a thing, guess when you see this word something clicks in your mind. Remember I told you that the inner you defines you, it also define your destiny in life, it doesn't need your looks or any helper but your determination and choices you make and for your choices to be good you have to proud of who you are first it doesn't take a day to do so but with patience you can make a good and valuable destiny that is meant for you and defines you.

ENTHUSIASTIC- As a person you have to have interest in yourself, eagerness and be motivated. If you have all that in your own recipe, it will make you something that everyone will respect and always want to be around. Showing interest in analysing yourself shows that you love yourself and want to know more about you as an individual, so be yourself and be proud. If you find it hard, try to look at yourself in the mirror and say "I love me" And that will motivate you to be enthusiastic.

FRAME- An open structure that gives you shape and supports you is the frame you put yourself in and whatever you choose will define you for who you are and make you unique from everyone else. So when you choose that frame make sure you fit in it because it should define you and make you proud. This not only your body but your state of mind as a person so that you can be independent and interested in yourself.

INTELLECTUAL- The capacity of understanding, thinking and reasoning is very important in a person's life. Now that brings a good characteristic, and for that I have realised most people fail in it because they are not true to themselves and doesn't know who they are. But if you learn to be honest you will find it easy my dear friend.

NATURAL- When speaking of nature we basically mean you not fake and you know where you come from and where you are going, the problem will arise when you are lost and living someone else's life. If you are natural you let people respect you and give yourself a good definition as you are showing the world that you love who you are. As a lady you have to be proud cause God was too, remember you have to fill someone's rib, so for that to be successful you have to work on being natural and realistic.

ELEGANT- As a lady I strongly believe we are all elegant as we are so tasteful in dress and style. We are cleverly simple than men and that is why we get labels like hot, you are a flower and etc. we need to love ourselves first to be tasteful. First know what kind of person you are, then what you like, what colours suit you, the type of body you have and what makes you feel brilliant in your own skin colour. And when you are sure of that hmm I am sure we will be able to see your own explanation, remember designers have sleepless nights trying to cover you all so don't disappoint them by being sour as you don't know what really defines you as a women, I know it is hard being women but we have to keep on trying to make it simpler.

TEE'S LOVELY EASY TIPS:

- Whenever you look at yourself in the mirror, say hi to yourself. That will bring self-love and a good self-esteem as you will know that before you love someone, love yourself and that you are unique and proud.
- Whenever you walk somewhere, it can be the mall, shop, or the streets, please walk with pride, you can even pretend as if you are at a catwalk and everyone is watching you. That will just show you are proud and love yourself just the way you are.
- When you feel like you are getting back to square one and having doubts that you are hot, honey go back to your mirror and repeat as much as you can and say '' I love me and I am proud of me''.
- Try to study yourself and understand yourself so that people can understand you too, because if you are confused then it is quite obvious you

won't be able to tell what is wrong with and that will confuse those around you.

- When you feel down and you are alone, just cry and take away that anger, use those tears when you are angry I promise you will find yourself relieved and make sure you tell yourself that you know you are capable and you know you are beautiful, look, don't wait for someone at the street to tell you that nah, do it first.

- When taking a shower touch yourself with pride and be proud of that body and get used to it because you can't let someone touch you while you are unhappy with your body, which makes those men abuse it as you already neglected it.

- Love your body and never let anyone pull you down, we will never look the same so we have to accept who we are, we can't have it all. You can even move around half naked, I do it too and that shows that you are happy don't be ashamed.

- Always remember that being true start in your heart, then the mind after it your actions that will say it all. Then you will be called miss independent, hmm how sweet!

- Don't hide yourself too much with makeup and weaves please at least try to be a little natural, we have to see that pretty face. No need to be afraid, God loves you, if your men tell you are not beautiful then just know he doesn't deserve you. Your moms have carried you for nine month for God sake, and then why try to hide that beauty?

- Being women simply means you must have your time alone, and bond with yourself that's a "me time", make yourself special and do your favourite thing. Try it its nice.
- Ever heard of self-acceptance? Now that one just tells you love who you are, no need for plastic surgery it will make things worse. What you can change is that bad character that people are scared of, you can make that dominant character to be recessive and be good.

Being a lady is not just a title no, it is a special name given to those who know how to look after it, cause that's what women are, special beings chosen by God to meet hardship but still be able to overcome it, so you can't just throw away a gold. You have to polish it, make it bright and put it at the dispensary. I know they say not all glitter is gold, but if you want to be a real one nothing is stopping you.

CHAPTER 2

MEN-Our Enemy

Have you realised that men can be our enemies sometimes that is why we find ourselves being the victims of different abuses every day. But now I think it's time to stop them, its 21st century, we got our rights and we are now given a chance to prove that we are capable, so we can't let men take that from us even now. Men need a woman of dignity, who thinks, who can speak for herself and a woman who can be a challenge. You know sometimes we women let this men undermine us and call us names because we don't love ourselves but still want to love them, do you seriously mean you will be respected that way? No think again, show your man you are not just a human being who doesn't know what she wants, prove to him that you are independent and you can do whatever you want yes we need them in our lives as partners but respect should be demanded, I am not saying disrespect your spouse, but when he want to make you feel like being around you it's a favour, then just tell him that he is not your type cause you deserve better than what he is delivering.

The word men brings a meaning to us women, let's look at this:

MOCKERS- Guess some of you were pulled down day by day by your partners, telling you that you don't deserve them, that you are cheap and that someone out there is better than you. Oh no that is emotional abuse, how will you love yourself and be safe in your own skin when someone is busy telling you how bad you are? Look you don't need a mocker in your life but you need a mentor, someone to be there for you. Partnership is about being together and helping one another in good and bad times, not being enemies in one room, men sometimes forget that as opposites we need each other in many ways and that is why we attract.

> **'Seems to me that men want to**
> **make angels of their wives**
> **Without first taking the trouble of**
> **making saints out of themselves,**
> – Henry Lawson

Those words made me realise that men expect us to be saints while they are not ready to be, it made me believe it because those words are said by a man. Being in a relationship is not about mocking and abusing each other but about complimenting each other, have fun and discuss your differences as a couple, and make sure you know each other's weaknesses and strengths, so that you can be good friends and be an ever fixed mark.

EGOTISTICAL- Ever had of egotism? Oh now that word sounds like a syndrome, and that syndrome is affecting most men out there. Some men just have an inflated sense of self- importance, self- centred, superiority or we can even say they are egocentric. Now that is a serious problem my friend, you know that if someone is selfish then that person is a parasite cause I know it is impossible to survive alone, no human can be an island I know, parasites benefit from a host but the host doesn't even benefit but it dies. Ladies aren't you tired of being hosts? Hey it's time to stop them. If your men is egocentric then you should be egomaniac and have obsessive love for yourself, give your man a challenge in a good way, show him you love yourself and that as a couple you need to purify your love. They are enemies sometimes but we can show them the right way out of love, it's not easy but always come with solutions that can make you feel good, remember you deserve to smile.

NUMPTY- Sometimes men can be so ignorant, and that's not healthy for a relationship, Dr David Molapo, a motivational speaker said what qualities women want in men very well, he said we want:

- A faithful man.
- A leader.
- A respectful man.

- A family man.
- A provider.
- An honest man.
- A man who she can communicate with.
- A man with sense of humour.
- A romantic man.
- A godly man.

After looking at this qualities you can realise that being a real man is not easy for them, but guess it's time they sit down and think about it before all real men die, they must know that we need them to know when we are good and bad, we need their attention. He doesn't really have to give his attention to sex only, a relationship needs communication, happiness and knowing each other, you have to connect so that nothing can come between your love and show each other real love, if you don't love each other but focusing on sex then better stop what you are doing cause sooner or later it will be over.

SUGAR DADDIES

'Dear admin my name is Lucy and I am 25, living in Seshego zone-4. I am dating a 55 years old man. Eish, we were living happily together and things started changing when we became pregnant with our baby, I tried in all means to be a loving wife but thing were worse as he even started beating me. I even had complications with my pregnancy and had a miscarriage too, go thata for me, but I don't want to go because I love him and without him I am nothing as I am jobless and my parents died recently. I can't leave him no, I am just stuck without him and I even don't have a matric certificate to get me a job. What must I do because he says he doesn't want his wife to work as we women undermine them when we are educated, I have had enough but there is nothing I can do. Please help.'

I guess some of you or someone you know was or is in this kind of situation, it is not a new story to you. Women, women we are given a chance to show the world that we are capable just like men but some ladies are still lazy to work for themselves and depend on sugar daddies, all I know is that things won't end well because this men know you are nothing without them. Young ladies just want to see themselves wearing Versace, Louis Vuitton, Prada and Dolce & Gabbana, drive lavish cars and live in mansions. Do we expect to get all that without working for them? Do you really think depending on someone is a solution while you don't have any qualifications? NO! Sugar daddies already lived their twenties and they enjoyed it but you are letting them ruin your fun because of lack of patience and wanting things you didn't work for, that's not good. Truly speaking I learned a lot from Kanyisile Mbau, I read a book written by Lesley Mofokeng titled '' BITCH PLEASE! I'M KHANYI MBAU'' I was forced to finish reading it because I once judged her, but after reading it I had a soft spot for her same time. You know why? That was because I listened to rumours and didn't even ask myself why she acted the way she did, so I read her story and learned a little from that person I undermined. From her story I realised that sugar daddies are not good for us, they trap us to a corner as they know we love money, and it comes easy for them to abuse us because we go to them being so dependent and we make many mistakes and regret after, truly speaking we are lucky to have Khanyi in our country, from her mistakes we can change the way we live this nowadays.

I liked her words when she said God allowed things that happened to her, to get her ready to face reality, after she doesn't care about clothes anymore. Wow doesn't that make her special, I personally respect her cause no matter how hard it was she still stood up for herself and became independent too, she learned from her mistakes and you can avoid mistakes by learning from her, remember many people are like angels to us, some even died and we benefited from their deaths, just like 'THE QUEEN OF BLING', we can learn from her and learn to stand up for ourselves and leave the old men to their peers, those people are like fathers to us, we need to have dignity as ladies, we have to stop sleeping with any man we meet in our lives, let them respect us by respecting ourselves, trust me on that one my friend, if you have dignity no one can try messing with you in a bad way, if anyone tries there must be a problem with one of the two.

THE SWEET GIRL IN BAD MOMENTS

It is good to be good and to smile but, sometimes you have to defend yourself when someone tries to attack you. Some girls are too bad out there and you will find everyone knowing that if you mess with her, you going to regret it. But find that her man is abusing her, she is always beaten and that she was once admitted in hospital. To be honest I will be shocked because I believe people living like her can't be abused.

I realised that some ladies out there can be bad in any way but they become good mamas when they are with their men, they try in all means to be sweet even if the guys are treating them bad. When the guy made a mistake you are letting him get away with it and you even say sorry when he is the one who is wrong, do you expect that person to be a good man to you? Haibo sisi! When your man is being bad to you show him you get angry too, you can even get out of the house to show him that he sometimes disgusts you, stop acting like a good girl in bad moments, you should give your man a challenge and make him realise when he fights you he will lose you one day, make him say sorry and buy you gifts to show how sorry he is, and if he beat you my dear you better pack your bags, don't let him repeat it again. A real lady wouldn't look at what people will say but will make her happiness come first, you are not a punching bag, if he tries to beat you, just tell him to go to the gym or even go to the ring and play what he is trying to do to you.

What I hate about sweet girls is that they don't even know how to say no, they will come to you and tell you how much they love their bad guys, some died because they loved their boyfriends more than the way they love themselves. Sweetie you rather be alone than to be unhappy. Stop finishing tissue while there are solutions, I know it is not easy but act before it is too late. You got to be louder than the silent killers, stop them from hurting some people again, and remember to love yourself my love.

WE STILL NEED THE ENEMY

The first thing you will ask yourself when you read my subtitle is what is their purpose? Well they do have a purpose without man we are nothing and they are nothing without us, I believe God created two sexes for a reason. We naturally need support, we want to hear good words and that's our definition, sometimes you just have to take out your frustrations on your partner and not on the children. I always look at my father busy with the garden at home and get to realise why my mother got married. Sleeping alone at night makes people think a lot but if you have a partner, you get to share all the bad things that happened that day, they can look like rubbish but at the end of the day they are a part of us, they are a shoulder that we can lean on in times of trouble. I know it sound like a contradiction, but truth has to be told, we still need them to open doors for us.

We get to see most successful, women looking all strong but we know deep inside they know a man is needed, all we have to learn is that it is not only about money, it is about being happy and keeping the love alive. Nothing beats happiness if you get to accept what you have and what you do, if we can keep on insulting them and saying they are bastards we will never get it right, why not try to change the way we see things and the way they see things, you can't love if you have no one to share it with.

THE BALLROOM DANCE

'Men initiates, women response,

In ballroom the man suggest a step but it is a woman's choice to accept it or deny it, you can give your partner the power but you still have that power against him, if you don't trust him then you are going to deny him the opportunity to lead you because you don't trust him. Dance is a tricky activity, you can practice for weeks but still does a mistake, that happens in life too, no one is perfect the enemy is not perfect and you are not too, learn from the mistakes and try new things, you can't give up on nice things because of silly mistakes. Just like ballroom dancing you have to learn to respect and trust each other and an element of etiquette and socialising cleverness. So give the enemy and yourself a chance. But remember respect is a must have and give situation. There is something we must always think, let's think of our future boys, they must grow up knowing that a man must respect his woman. By that I mean if we can counterattack men who don't really give respect, then we will be saving the world and the future. Remember the world needs strong women with visions.

TEE'S TIPS...

- Don't let men take you for granted, if you had enough just pack you bag and leave him behind cause surely he doesn't deserve you. Real men must not make his women cry but be her shelter.

- Try in all means to be miss independent, which makes men respect you. But if you become a beggar you are letting people undermine you and disrespect you. You have to show people you can do it yourself. You are your own boss lovey.

- Let them know that they should respect you the way they wanted their fathers to look after their mothers, because if he treats you badly your children will be affected in the future.

- As a woman you should show your partner that this world doesn't evolve around him, cause that will affect his relationship with you.

- As partners you should be a team, and be beside each other no matter what, because surely you need each other and to share this life together but if you are failing to do so, things won't be good. Mother Teresa once said, 'If we have no peace, it is because we have forgotten that we belong to each other'. So you don't have to undermine each other but give support, advises and trust because no man is an island.

- Learn to communicate about many things just like a team, remember Barcelona wouldn't be a great team in UEFA if there wasn't any communication. So take your relationship with your loved one as team and work on taking your love to the top by making each other smile, no matter the distance away.

- Play your part in a relationship and keep spicing it with new formulae, so that it wouldn't get boring.
- If you have kids it doesn't mean it is the end of your love. No! You have to love each other just like before, keep in mind that weights, heights, age and your hair will eventually grow old but your hearts will never change if you don't let useless things change it.

CHAPTER 3

THE X-AXIS (INDEPENDENT VARIABLE)

At school I always knew that when I am drawing my graph I have to have the x and y axis, and that on the y-axis it is the dependent variable and x axis it is the independent which is the ones that don't change on my graph. But that gave me an idea that as a person I have to fight to be like my x axis as they are a fixed variable and avoid being changed. In life you have to be yourself and show your character with no fear cause if you change the real you then you will be around people who you will not enjoy their company, that is because you will find friends of your new character not for the person in you, so it is important to be an ever fixed mark my dear friend, don't be the subject to be controlled by others, beware of being reliant it is not good at all.

I like emphasising independence because I have realised that most people don't know when to say "yes" or "no", it just come hard for them to make choices and expect others to do that for them. You were once the fastest sperm hey, don't tell me the sperm just ran for nothing my friend, we all came in one manner to this world so really nobody is too clever to own your life unless you let them. I always tell my friends that I do things my way because when I face the consequences I don't have to blame them.

IF YOU MAKE YOUR OWN CHOICES, YOU WONT HAVE REGRETS.

Life is all about choices, it needs your skill to make it smooth because naturally it's rough, and yeah we won't use one method but can still do the best out of it, remember there are many ways to kill a cat that's because it is not selfish it just need your attention. The secret is that life gives you back what you put in it, all you have to do is to be careful and always make sure you make your dream become a reality, I know it is not easy but just one step at a time as the great singer Jordan Sparks said in her song that one step at the time, there is no need to rush, she was right cause if you rush into things you end up taking short cuts which will make you take wrong choices in your life. There is a proverb that I still live by which says 'diligence is the mother to fortune' meaning hard work and industry is key to success and great achievements. Do not depend on short cuts or sheer luck. They say we must learn from our mistakes but I want to say just avoid mistakes other people did, I am saying this because we sometimes get lucky and meet people who made their mistakes and we get a chance to avoid them and learn from them, I know it is not easy but if we can look at it in a positive way we will realise that some people's mistakes can make us do good choices. In this world we are here to learn from each other and to help one another, even if you fighting to be on the X-axis put in mind that there will always be a Y-axis to rate you, and in that way you learn and become a better person. I personally learned a lot from my parents, family, siblings and friends' even strangers and that makes me be able to analyse most of the things I do. Making choices can be tricky sometimes because you will find that your mind believe what you are doing is right while your heart doesn't or vice versa, it is normal but before you take your choice just look deeply into it and you will be able to choose whether your heart or mind is right for that situation. There are some people who get into traps and when you ask them how it all happened, they will tell you they thought what they did was right, you know why that happens? That is because we sometimes do things out of excitement, to please somebody, not understanding the situation and taking wrong advises from people.

THE RADIO

We all get and need advises from people around us, but sometimes the advises might not be the way you expected them to be, they may not be convincing as much, but as an individual you shouldn't force yourself to do things based on other peoples rules or past experiences but by your own self-satisfaction. A good example of this is a radio, it has presenters who work on a fixed programme, and the listeners can't change it even if they don't like it, but rather they can change the station. Just like you, nobody should try to choose what you must do for yourself, imagine how it would feel like if you listened to some advice that put you in danger while you know you had a better idea than the one you were told to do, I mean it should be up to you, you can make your own choices just like your radio broadcaster so that nobody controls you, be the broadcaster of your own life. It's a tricky task but you can accomplish it if you can put your spirit to it, all you need is your soul, body, emotions and your mind. Taking that as your team for your radio station, obviously you will have listeners who are interested in your broadcast and appreciate what you offer. I sometimes tell people that I don't believe in dreams but I believe in goals, and someone responded and said "but they are not that different" my answer was that goals have a deadline and dreams don't, if your life is not stable you won't know when you've reached the peak of your goals, planning and sticking to what you believe in is not a child's play but it needs all the tools that I mentioned above, remember your listeners believe in you, maybe you asking yourself who will be interested in what you trying to accomplish or achieve, but I want to remind you of something, your parents and siblings will always be interested, they take a big part of you. There are some whom envy from a distance and really love what you have made up of your life, rather focus on those positive admires than those that believe you're a waste of time

BE THE DEAF FROG

There is an interesting story my friend once told me, he said in life you have to be deaf like the deaf frog at that time I was unable to relate, what happened is that the frogs were having a race and while they were racing the other frogs on the side of the road were busy making noise and discouraging the racers that they won't make it to the finish line as it is impossible, saying the one which can get there would have made history, what happened is that the frogs quit the race one by one but the was still one which did not lose focus, they all quitted the race except that one frog, when it reached the finish line, all those frogs came to it, praising it but it never responded, that was because it couldn't hear the others. So my lovely friends you see, it was not impossible the only problem was with the supporters who discouraged the racers and the problem is that the racers listened to them and didn't test their ability, the y axis took over them. This short tale just means in life we tend to listen to the negativity people bring to us, we never even test our strengths before we give up, remember be independent and stick to what you believe in, if you want to do something go for it maybe that is the right way to go.

LET'S ANALYSE INDEPENDENT:

IMPLICITY- if you are implicit I believe you know what you are doing without doubt or reserve, you look in what you believe in and take it with both hands, and if you can decide to be like that then hmmm, no human being will ever try to take over your life. You will be a mark that cannot be erased, just like our x-axis

NATURAL- I had to find a good explanation on how to make this easy for you to understand, the definition said nature closely resembles an original, meaning you won't try to be an artificial you, because you have to fit in or maybe because you hate your life. What I want you to learn so far is that, just know nature is what you should believe in, know what your roots are and understand why you are you and why is it good to be you.

DISJUNCTION- is a sharp cleavage, or maybe a separation. One might say why did I choose a word like this well, remember the say that" the disjunction between theory and practice". Yup that, we all get a lot of theory about life and how is the best way to live it but the practicing is different and by that you will get the separation of what you believe in and what you should do, so my lovely friend, what is your theory that you believe in and how are you going to practice that? That is your little homework which you will try to look into and answer it, that's a rhetorical question by the way.

EAGER- if you are eager to do something or maybe interested in something, nothing can change your mind and that's what I want you to learn. When you are eager you will be enthusiastic and ready for any challenge. That's what a real goal maker is; they are eager to meet the deadline and will overcome any challenge because what is important is the finish line.

PATIENCE- when someone is patient, we can say that person is not hasty or <u>impetuous</u>. Remember you are passionate but not in a hurry, remember no shortcuts in life because you might end up in danger, so, always take the paved roads with the right speed.

ENORMOUS- We all have those enormous dreams in our lives but maybe the cost is high or maybe we are just lazy to take them, my dearest friend life is about thinking big and dreaming big, never underestimate yourself, there is no human being who is better than the person in you, we all different and all have different abilities. Take advantage of the fact that you are different, it works for me; imagine what it can do for you.

NEATEN- in life no man is perfect and if there was, lord knows it would be tough for some people to be alive, I am going to contradict my statement by saying, even if you not perfect, why not try to be neat, neat in a manner that your life is in order and has less complications, goal setters make sure their life is in the right way and try to be neat, not that you have to be perfect but at least be in order for the sake of yourself, it's the right thing. Try it.

DEVELOP- I sometime joke with friends and say in life you have to do things in high levels, development is just what every person need, I always get surprised when I go to a place after 5 years and nothing has changed, or maybe meeting an old friend and nothing has changed.

When I get home I sit down and ask myself is this place going to be like this forever? Or is this person dead while inhaling oxygen. Life is about development and that is why I think you have to set goals and try to be somewhere in life, not in one place. NO.

ENTITY- being, existence; independent, separate, or self-contained existence, entity has a big meaning with six letters right? Yeah I am now just trying to emphasis my chapter about independence because really, I hate it when I see my sisters and brothers out there relying so much on other people, can't we at least be the generation to break the chain? Let's try it; maybe we could make the change.

NUANCE- this is the kind of word I would say you should try to describe your radio with, you will bring meaning to all your feelings and most of all what you believe in, remember the listeners are forced to listen to the sweetness of your variation, it is never too late to try and be the best broadcaster.

TIP-IN- do you sometimes watch basketball? Well tip-in it is a goal which is scored in a very close range. Don't confuse my tip-in with short cuts but know that in life if you get an opportunity, grab it with both hands and never let go of it. Sometimes when you take safe chances you might find that you got your goal before the deadline.

CHAPTER 4

STANDARDS, STATUS AND SHOWING-OFF (SSS) THE TRIPLE "S"

It is every girls dream to be a queen when she grows up, but some overdo it in a bad way, I personally wished I could at least get a man who can do everything for me but I sat down and rephrased my statement and said I want to be able to do everything for myself.

"Trying to live a life that you don't afford, is like taking a rope and hanging yourself for no valuable reason"
– Thekgo

I seriously get it that no human want to live low and be undermined but my question is, do you think of your reputation and your future or maybe what kind of a mark you want to leave on earth, I get it we have always heard people tell us that we should keep shooting for new and loftier goals, but seem like we misinterpreted what it really means. This doesn't mean go around gambling with your life for money to meet the standard. I once read a piece on Google by Jody Prince it stated that, a lot of men want to be needed by a woman, to make them feel like man, off which is true, they want to own you and supress your mind, I am not trying to turn you against them but I wish they should know you are a treasure to your parents too.

Sometimes the things we do are just taking us back without realising it, it's really a step backwards but it becomes invisible because we are desperate and hungry for wealth which we didn't work for, you can't just jump in a car you don't even know how much its deposit was or how the person got the money to buy it. We really have to think sometimes, honestly men in expensive cars attract me too, but before I try to do something stupid, I think about it and avoid the damage it might cause for me. We are human and temptations will always be there, but I believe an attractive woman is the one who has dreams, is self-orientated and knows what she wants than a woman who just sit down and wait for a man to show her the purpose of life.

THE TRUTH

I have been looking and trying to understand what really men look into when they meet a woman, it is an opinionated situation with different answers based on how we observed it. But personally I think what most men care about is how a woman looks like, to be there as their trophy to show off and play around with you around friends in clubs and pubs, but my questions is do you feel good for being like that or it is just a trap you found yourself in? I sometimes observe pretty women in restaurants with their boyfriends, who are in businesses you find that the lady doesn't have a say, all she does is smile and eat, maybe go to the bathroom to check if the makeup is fine, this doesn't mean they don't have brains, no I totally disagree. I personally don't believe in the saying that some woman are just pretty but have no brain, there is no such. If you ready to crack the shell of hiding who you are, you will see how incredible you are.

YOUR HAPPINESS

This high standards are keeping most women from happiness, you may not be doing the laundry, cooking and etc. but most of the time you are not happy, that is because you made wrong choices thinking if you are depending on someone all will be well but forgetting in the eyes of that person you are a fool and you will become his stress ball, when things go wrong, it will always be your fault and even if you find him cheating or maybe doing something you don't really like you won't be able to do anything because you are trapped in someone else's court, and it is because you sold yourself low and you are now stuck. Is that what you want or you just didn't think it would be like that? You may look pretty and have everything but imagine what might happen if the man decides to leave you, you have to start over again before people start realising that you are no longer sleeping in bling's and that you are now a loner because all that you had is gone, guess what you will do next, sooner or later you will be sleeping with anything that breathes and stands erect, it won't be because you want to but because you are forced, want to know why? Because you have to meet the standard again, remember you have to rise from the dead to stop people talking.

YOUR TYPE

We always try to persuade people that we don't know what are the kind of ladies that certain man goes for, but honestly we could see, looking at the way they talk and live their lives, if you are going to try to fit in then it's going to be a tough one, if you are going to sacrifice the person in you to fit in a man's life then I feel sorry for you, he is going to change you bit by bit and at the end you are going to realise that you don't know who you are, you are just a lost sheep in the jungle which doesn't know where home is. You will have to keep up with the pretension and the skills to hide that you are not happy. There will be a point where you are going to be confused, that's going to make you think you don't deserve any good men, remember before you felt like this you just adhere to the highest standards you never thought of its consequences. And you will realise that your level of fulfilment has fallen drastically, with no good results. Remember if you don't undermine yourself and knowing what man deserves you then, it will be easy to see men who go with who you are, and you will realise that some men out there are suited to your lifestyle and believes. Maybe you expect more but I strongly believe what is important is to know that you mean a lot to someone.

THE RESPECT YOU DESERVE

Maybe you don't know but let me remind you, before you think of the triple's" think about what you deserve as woman. I am one person who really demand respect from all my male friends, not because I am trying to make myself look better but because I know I deserve it as a young woman, I am not a welcome mat at the door that every person need to clean his shoes before getting somewhere in life, and I expect you not to allow that too. I believe a man should see that you are a woman, by that I mean he should know that respect is your #1 priority, he must know you don't just jump in any car, and if he is lucky to give you the lift, then he must open the door for you, ladies that is the beginning of respect. I always tell my friends that love and respect goes hand in hand, you can't say you love someone while you don't respect that person. But, but remember something too, you can't demand respect while you don't respect yourself. Respect is earned, I believe any person will love you so long as you love and respect yourself. Raise the bar for our own sake to make people realise that you are a real young woman, and try not to do things that are an insult to the kind of life and respect you want.

THE GOLD DIGGER

This is a trending topic because we sometimes don't see if it love or the girl is still with the man because of the man's money. I once saw a post of some girl on Facebook saying, if men marry for beauty then why women can't be equally materialistic and marry for money. It got over 200 comments because it was kind of interesting. Well I know some man spoil a woman with the money that they think is worth their looks, well that I can't argue but throwing your life away because you have the looks and can get any tycoon, what I know is you don't believe in love and being happy then these financially contingent relationship will work, I personally rather walk in Oprah's shoes than being someone's show off in exchange for money, why are you still waiting for someone to make you rich instead of doing it yourself? I am not trying to play perfect but I don't see the use.

There is nothing wrong for us to expect men work for our good looks and provide us with what we need in the affair of partnership and support, whether its financial or not but in everything there is a balance of give and take, what I mean is that you must know what you want, don't be around because of money while you not happy. Remove the gold-digger mind-set and set a goal in a relationship, whatever you believe in should be expressed. If you can know what you want in a relationship, then most of you would have succeeded in meaningful and respected relationships, I know they might be dogs but sometimes the ball is in our courts were we get to choose what we want over money. Look at all those wealthy athletes and models who keep marrying and divorcing because their men all think their wives are with them because of money, sometimes it is not that and we get to find that men are pushing their soul mates away. I personally know that I will choose to be in love and if that means working from 9am to 5pm I don't mind. I am not saying I don't want a provider in my life, what I mean is that we should meet one another halfway, as most believe that money must be the deciding factor for us women to do what they say, I still want to be myself and that's a chance I can't take, of missing out on what I want to achieve because of some else's money. I guess you don't want to be someone's show piece, so make your mind take a U-turn and take a good decision.

CHANGING INTO A GOAL-DIGGER

We are now going to tackle the issue of setting a goal, you are going to learn to be a person that is passionate, has integrity, and ready to take smart moves. You will start everything from the scratch without digging gold. Instead of hunting a rich person you will learn to create your own goals and turn yourself into an x-axis, so that when the y-axis comes along you will be ready to have a say and stay unchangeable, it's good to find a helper when you already started a foundation.

STEPS TO FOLLOW WHEN YOU WANT TO BE A GOAL-DIGGER:

- **Set a goal:** There is always a start for everything, everything starts with a thought and then action will follow. You have to for see what you want to achieve, picture it, analyse it and then come up with a schedule to make it happen. It is like trying to save money in the bank for a certain project, you don't have to temper with until the day you planned to withdraw it and use it. Remember every goal must have a deadline so that the goal won't be procrastinated.
- **Be persistent:** I guess up until now you have been hearing and still hearing that you must not give up, what I have proven from what I have read about giving up is that, we tend to give up when we are about to get to what you have been working for a while now. So try to hold on and tell yourself you are going to score this goal when the keeper is not expecting it
- **Believe yourself:** Be confident of what you want to get, you can't face the goal keeper if you are scared and not confident that you can face him. It all starts in the mind and if the mind is sharp

then nothing can let you down. Sometimes we don't have to test our abilities but have to believe then. If you were used to sitting down and do nothing because you think you are good at that, then I want to unwrap it to you that there is more to that if you can just stand up and take a step and you will be shocked of what you are capable of. Whatever article of faith you have, you will get the results from that.

- **Compete yourself:** Competition will never be healthy no matter how we try to modify it, I am saying this because it never motivates but brings jealousy and hatred, but if you can be your own opponent then nothing will pressurise you and you will do everything according to your own pace. Try being your own motivation, try being jealous of yourself, that way you will be bringing peace in your life and making things easier for yourself, and avoiding distraction for what you want to achieve. Being a goal digger is about learning to know that your journey is yours alone and so you have to motivate yourself and get it through your mind that you are a believer and you will get the goal, in your own terms and pace.

- **Acknowledge yourself:** We don't always need people to be the ones who will pat us on our shoulders when we achieved something, before they do you have to look in your mirror and smile to yourself and say "you have done good", keep yourself going, let their congratulations be some bonus point, this is for you and if you have done great you should be the first to see that. Be the first one to recognise it because you are the one who did set the goal. Even if it doesn't look the way you wanted it to be, at the end of the day it is a progress, you have moved from one place to the other.

- **Derive yourself:** you can get anything you want by pushing yourself forward, get your wishes granted through hard work and believe, learn to stand up and see where your few foot-steps will take you. Before you start judging yourself and stopping to push first try and you will be surprised of what you can do. What you have to make sure is that you push and push until you get the results, that goal wasn't set by anyone but yourself so it is your duty to make it happen. And remember goal diggers are there to dig harder no matter how sweaty or tiring it could be, if you really and seriously need something, you will give it your all. Keep digging your goal until you get it, your sweat will surely give you what you want. Remember you are the only one who can make that happen.

WHAT RESPECT HAS FOR US:

REPUTE- If you know what you want, you know what you doing then that don't means nothing can change the things you repute in, not all gold is glitter.

If you want that gold, go dig for it yourself, if you want a tower you have to build it for yourself. And remember you have all the tools.

EMERGE- you have to be able to rise for yourself if you want to be something in life, it is important to set your life high that it surprises those who thought you will never be anything in life. Remember we all have enemies who wish we can take the wrong way, but at least surprise them and show them you can do it all by yourself. Rise high and be your own warrior.

SPECULATE- Life is about speculation, we foresee things before they happen. Before all the innocence was taken away you had a dream, you knew what you wanted. As I said temptations will be there but you have to try to avoid them because they are the obstacles blocking your success, I believe in you and I hope you do the same too.

PROGNOSTICATE- I believe every person vaticinate their lives and picture how they will be in that time, that is a good thing to do but my question is are you picturing the right things, are you ready to take the race of life? Do you believe you can do this? Yes I do, the only problem now is when are you going to start, you have vaticinated all and painted the picture, the only thing missing is believe. You are able to do all the things you saw yourself do in your dreams.

EQUABLE- in life I believe you should be stable, know what you want and know where you stand, sometimes you find someone always changing and everywhere, you may find the person is this today and tomorrow the other, now that is not good. Life is about order and stability, if you forgot you can still go back and understand why I say equability is important.

CONN- every ship needs a conductor and in this case let's takes your life as a ship and you are the conductor, who controls where it goes and where it will end, you don't have to let anyone show you the road cause I believe you won't steer it if you don't know the directions yet.

TOSS-UP- are you still in an undecided situation whereby you don't really know what you want yet? Well it is not late for change, if you really have varieties I would advise you to toss – up and by that I mean you have to analyse each and everything, know why is it good for you, why you want to do it and why it is the best choice. You can still tabulate your facts and choose the best one based on your abilities and character.

CHAPTER 5

ABUSE

When the world takes over your life you get to wonder what is it that you did wrong, I know you try so hard to talk that you being abused but you are frequently threatened that they will kill you, but my dear how long are you going to hold the pain inside you. Don't you think it's time you talk and see your freedom?

There is no true facts about why some men have the courage to lay a hand on a woman, or maybe try to make the woman feel little, I know most of the time we tend to blame ourselves but honestly the problem is not with you but with that enemy you are living with or maybe dating. To be clear I want to tell you that if you find a man trying to degrade you then it means he has his own personal issues, he is trying to make himself better by seeing you suffer, maybe you sometimes ask yourself is this person human or an animal, well, he is human but acting like an animal.

'Abuse doesn't just start, it starts with a silly thing and then it grows into something serious. You will only notice when you now trapped and out of ideas,

Well what the quote mean above is that, before a person lay a hand on you he will test your reaction, he might just push you with his finger on your forehead and say "you fool" and that might make you think he is just angry but no that is the beginning, there is still more coming, next he will say he hates your friends and your family, which will make sense at that time but you just forgot that the people who will forever be on your side are your friends and family. Abuse has its own stages, so I would advise that if you see symptoms of abuse, it is time to move on. You can't be stuck because of kids or maybe some life you always dreamt of, I don't think that is a smart move because honestly, he is going to kill you, and not in a normal death but in tragic one, you may think stress or a heart attack will kill you but the truth is he is going to kill you with his bare hands, an at that time it would be too late.

SYMPTOMS OF AN ABUSIVE RELATIONSHIP

This is what you will see in a man who is mostly likely to abuse you and hurt you.

- Low self-esteem

- Doesn't trust you
- Jealous when he sees you with other men
- Hate seeing you socialise with your male colleagues
- Always checking your phone and your work schedule
- Controls who you must speak to
- Sometimes he shows that he can't believe you in his life
- Always stalking you when you out with friends

There is still a lot more but these are the few that most woman see when something is wrong with their men, when someone is beating you and hurting you that is not love, it is just a decision he choose to boost himself, you may find that when he is with other men out there he is one of the stupidest people and because of that, he tries to man up when he is with you. Some of the things I have realised is that most are good with women outside, you may find that whenever you try to report him to your friends, they may tell you the problem is with you, as your man is good and knows how to treat women, they always say not guilty till proven guilty but we must remember we don't know what happens behind closed doors. I believe speaking and letting others know what you are going through is something you should consider.

<u>JEALOUSY</u>

Jealousy might look like love when you just fallen in love, but there is some which is just too much, you find that the person want you to be an island, I know when it's still new, it will surely look romantic for some but that is one of the symptoms of abuse.

It starts as "what were you doing with that man, are you cheating?" and you will be like "ohh nchooh you jealous, not knowing the king is mad and ready to roar at you anytime soon, I once watched a movie entitled insecure, the man really shown how obsessed he is about time, even if the lady is a minute late that was disrespectful to him. Sometimes it is not your fault, sometimes it's the guy's fault, because of how he was raised and told as a child. It is not just women who need to be shown love but any person should be shown love, whether you a guy, girl, man or a woman. And people you claim you love shouldn't be scared around you; they should feel safe and know they can trust you. If you sometimes scaring them you are shaking the trust

I used to meet girls who saw beating as a romantic thing, thinking the guy cares and beats them for their own good, because he doesn't want her to be in danger but the woman not seeing that she is already around danger, at that time it might be a slap but next it will be a fist then a kick and then next they will be combined and you will get killed for someone's' insecurities, let me make it clear for you yes you may be in love with the man but sometimes if those you love don't show you love, why don't you give those who love you a chance? You may say the guy doesn't meet your needs and standards but find that he will treat you like a queen your mom believes you are.

GETTING HELP

The first step to get help is having the courage to talk and seek guidance, I know you were always threatened that they will kill you but don't you think you have to act before he does something to you? I know you are scared of him because he has shown you that he is capable of killing you but then sweetie before it is too late I think you have to act, get out of the shell, be a free bird and live your normal life again, you may think it's over but it is not over till you lose your last breath, I know it is not an easy task but you will surely get out of this, first of all I am going to tell you I believe in you and I need you to help in making the world a better place.

We are living in a generation which many young girls lack self-esteem and worry too much of how they look, how are we going to take on the guys if we don't have self-love? That is the first step from stopping them from abusing us and undermining us. I know most young girls think looks are the ticket to a successful life but the truth is it won't give you anything and beauty won't take anything because beauty is nothing, I am going to tell you a little secret about myself, I am the ugliest woman alive and I love it, you know why? Because it pushes me forward, and again with this ugly features I have I still get boys coming to me, because it's not about my beauty only, but my personality and my confidence around them. I can stand for myself and won't let them disrespect my body or me. I love the way I am and how I look, it may not be a definition of beauty but because of how I look, I am me, what I do in my own way is the definition of me, see? If you think you are ugly then I think it's time you acknowledge that, it is the definition of you, life is not about beauty but hard work and patience. If you are not ready then I am not going to rush you but we have to fight abuse and turn it around to:

- **A**mbition- has a desire to achieve a certain goal.
- **B**lessing- you are a blessing to your mom and dad, they will always love you no matter what, keep that in mind.
- **U**niqueness- you are beautiful in your own way, the way you look is the definition of yourself, learn to accept your looks
- **S**atisfaction- be satisfied with what you have and never lower yourself for goods, love will find you not the other way around.
- **E**motionalize- give emotional quality to yourself.

THE PERSON IN THE MIRROR

Sometimes when you look in the mirror you might hate what you see, sometimes our reflections might disgust us. We all have those moments whereby we feel sad, happy, lonely or maybe peaceful and when those times comes there is a different way you are going to look in that mirror, obviously when you angry you will look ugly, who want to be ugly? I believe it's no one and when you happy you will glow and see that beautiful side of yourself. I know we are used to hearing it from people but why don't we do it by ourselves for a change, at least once a day tell the person in the mirror you love her and that you will never allow anyone mess with her.

Let me tell you something if you didn't know, love starts within and it is expressed out by a smile and the good actions people see, no human being could try to let you down if you already strong minded and loving that unique person you are. The mirror is the opponent that will always have your back no matter what, that person in the mirror is a constant reminder that you are alive and you should live life, I personally sometimes feel sad and down but I always take my mirror and smile, then say "it is good to be alive, some people didn't get the chance today but I did; want to know why? I am appreciating what God has given me and that is life, people who die every day will never have a chance to see themselves in the mirror and see their reflection. I always say the mirror is my psychologist. It helps me see the inner me and it helps me see the mistakes I have before going out, I love it because it repeats what I say, and remember as life is an echo. I have realised it should be my best friend.

I believe if you are satisfied and happy to see that person in the mirror it will not be easy for anyone to try to let you down and I believe if you have the confidence no one will do any shit to you. I love life and I respect myself, so I would love it if you could do the same. our actions won't be perfect but if we could try to live life in a safer way that will be a good way to avoid the predators which are out there trying to destroy us, and remember life is about doing it for yourself, if you do it yourself, you won't throw it away easy.

LET US LOOK AT THE MEANING OF OUR MIRROR:

Marvellous

Impactful

Respectable

Risible

Openhearted

Rarity

Look on the positive side because your uniqueness count and we need it in this world, we were all born for different purposes, they might not look visible now but keep pushing and look for them, that little thing you are good at can help the world. Change the world and make it a better place for everyone including yourself.

CHAPTER 6

THE ROUGH DIAMOND

**'Let your disabilities be recessive and
dominate your inner strengths,**

Maybe you are lost and don't know what you want to
do and what you want but then I am going to help you
realise what you are, you are a rough diamond that is not
yet processed. You may not be shining today but surely
we have to work on the layers that are covering your
potential.

What I know is that every person have a different
account of his/her journey, a different past and a different
road, we are here as a cycle and we are connected,
every person in this world has a purpose that has to be
accomplished, we are unique because we will be able to
invent the balance generation to generation. Just because

your sister or brother is a doctor doesn't mean you should be one. Make your own choices and believe in them, break the shell. The most important thing you should remember is that don't judge anyone, whatever you think is cheap or maybe not your standard, to God it is a big thing, people have the choices they made because they had an adventure that you will never understand, the least you can do is to respect the balance on earth.

The layers I am referring to are the negative thoughts, the hate, the wrong choices and the wrong strategies. We are all able in the eyes of the lord and our loved ones, we may not see our purpose yet but then let me remind you of something. When you were born, your little hands were closed. They were not just closed but there were duties in them, God sent you here to bring something, we are a lot of people but each and every one of us has a duty he or she must finish or deliver before we die, the secret of life is that we are not learning to live but to die because in this world we have purposes and after that there comes a time to leave earth and go live an eternal life.

The layers are stopping you to shine and be you but I think it's time to work on that and be the diamond I believe in, yuppie.

Yes an unpolished and a rough diamond appear like a dull piece of glass. Only when it is polished and processed, it will be sparkling good, shining and showing different colours in the sun. So let's relate to you as well, if you are I believe you just need a bit of polishing and processing, then you will be good, here are the steps on how a diamond is processed.

I had to find out how it is processed to help you change too and this is what I found

PROCESSING OF A DIAMOND

- **Drawing/marking**- when a diamond is being changed from raw to jewellery, STEPS are taken and the first is drawing, the processers mark the diamond in order to find how they are going to cut it so that it can look good. So as you will be the processer of your own, first you are going to mark and select the good things you are good at and those are the ones you are going to focus on. Then you have to jot down your strengths and draw out a plan of what you want in life.
- **Cleaving/sawing-** cleaving is a method of splitting a diamond parallel to the direction of the crystal grain with a single blow, this is a part were they break it into pieces to remove the impurities. So now my processor you are going to start looking on the positive side and then look deeply if you don't have any impurities in them and the first impurity is if you are still negative, now it is time to be ready for a good start and if you really want to be a better person, the first thing you are going to work on is that mind. The mind plays a big role in our lives so, please be positive minded and remove those irregularities, remember you must be sparkling no dull.

- **Bruting-** this is the shaping part of the base of the diamond, now you are going to shape yourself, your mind and your actions. This is serious business remember, what you must do is look at the base which is the beginning which I believe is today, you are going to be fit socially, mentally, emotionally and spiritually. Remember your wellbeing is the beginning of a bright future, just like the diamond darling you are going to fix all the problems that are stopping you from shining and then think positively too. If you still alive you can make it.

- **Polishing-** now this is the final step were they process it to be sparkling and nice, that's where the facets of the diamond is done. So you are now positive and ready for any challenge I guess and you are going to break the shell, you went through the steps as the diamond and now you are shining and ready to go, again I am going to say it again. I believe in you so I hope you do the same, you are worth it just like that diamond, remember it is expensive and you are too hey.

I believe after following those steps of a processing of a diamond you will look just like it and you will shine after that because the only problem was the layers covering you.

<u>WHERE IT ALL WENT WRONG</u>

All children are naturally confident and they are always glowing and incandescent. They do what they want and if they want something they do and grab it, it can be a piece of a toy but if they fell in love with it they will try to get it. Even if they didn't get it at least they tried and sometimes they get them. They get so strategic to get what they want and try to change their parents' minds.

We are all like that but as we grow as I told you it becomes a bit uptight, we find that we are no longer the deaf frogs and we listen to peers and take short cuts, and sometimes some start trying to impress people than going to take what they always dreamt of, the confidence is lost too and the self-love to. Some of you start thinking you are unattractive and ugly and when looking in that mirror you don't smile like the time you were a kid, were you would always smile when looking at the reflection of yourself. Now at this time you feel like you are not that bright diamond you once were before, but you are forgetting that when you start acting in that way then you are slowly changing the lovely processed diamond into being rough again. I know sometimes it is friends and the opposite sex who can make you feel down, maybe the friends always say you are not good and you need to transform and be like them, and then the boys are maybe not that interested in you and asking you out like other girls you refer as "hot".

Now those were also the layers covering your potential, only if you knew that was pulling you back but then again, it is not yet late because you are now going to get a chance to transform into a better individual who is striving for a better life for your kids and yourself.

LET US NOW LOOK INTO THE MEANING OF DIAMOND

Decent- you are a decent person and you have always been. It was just the little challenges in your life that covered you with a shell to think you are not decent, now I am really proud to say you are decent as ever and all will be well.

Important- you are important and the world needs you too, some may not see your use but you mean a lot to some of us, because we know no man was born without any duties.

Amazing- you are amazing in your own way and that is what is important, believe in yourself and respect yourself because you are incredibly ama-zing.

Meaningful- you have a purpose and that counts, remember we are taking on the world so that it can be a better place. You really mean a lot and if you are down please sit back and remind yourself that you are worth it.

Opportune- you are significant and lovely in your own way. Being original is the way it is done and that is what is needed all you need is to be yourself and know your uniqueness define you. So you are suitable for being around and helping making the change. It is time we change the mind set of negativity. The world needs us.

Needful- you are needed and it is time to do the duties God brought you to do, if you are still able to wake up in the morning, there is still something you still have to do. Why are you still trying to bury your potential when we need it?

Different- I always emphasis on uniqueness and because that defines you then it is the way to go. You are the best just the way you are, you don't need any corrections.

NEVER GIVE UP

The person in you is stronger than you think, there are many people who were told or thought that they won't make it in life but let me tell you something look up to them because they took the negative words and built something big out of them, while they are still trying to pull you down the only thing you must do is believe in you, tell yourself that it is not over till the last breath. The only appropriate excuse you have to give up is when you are dead. Keep trying and moving forward. The possibility of you absorbing something the first time you do it is slight, all things take time and mistakes happen along the way, all you need to do is learn from them.

You are stronger than you think, you can't give up because of one thorny road, neither big serious setback don't have to stop you from getting there, you will achieve what you want to get, failing is when you giving up, but attempting again shows courage and passion, even if you are the inventor of that dream, nothing should make you give up. Believe in your dreams and don't ever let anyone try to annihilate your dreams. There are people out there who are going through worse situations than you, think of those who want to move on but can't because they are in comas and having sicknesses that are stopping them from going forward. The little you do brings a difference to our future and the world too.

You are able to face yourself in the mirror every morning right, now it is time to face your fears, I taught you how to process the diamond you are, so now it's your time to decide whether you are ready to shine or not, wouldn't it be a good thing to be an inspiration to the people around you, try to be the reason people don't give up because they looked up to you, we get to give up when we very close to the destination, yes it might look like it has been long but why give up after all those years? Now this is going to sound crazy but just don't give up because I am telling you so, as I have already told you I believe in you. Now make a favour and believe in you, you will see miracles.

CHAPTER 7

SUICIDE

I am not going to judge those who already took their lives, but I am going to try to stop you if you are maybe trying to take your life. Don't you think it's a bit selfish? Don't you think you are going to leave people and most of all your family with many question marks and unanswered questions? Do you know how much you are loved and how much some people need you?

Those are just a few questions I can ask and I hope you will answer them before you take those pills, poison or that rope in your hand.

I always believed in talking and writing. We all have problems we think we can't handle but only to find that it is nothing at all, God gave you the life and he should be the one to decide when to take it. People are crowded in hospitals, people going to church, people going to traditional healers and some even go miles away from the country, want to know why? They are fighting for their lives. Even though it is a dangerous thing that might disadvantage them they still go, just too at least see the next day. When I first heard of the scenario that happened in Nigeria were the building fell and people lost their lives, I honestly judged and said why would people just leave their home and go to some church which is not guaranteed that they will get the help they need, and later on I realised, I would do anything to safe my life. We should cherish every minute of our lives and we should fight for it and not try to cease it.

I once heard a quote saying "some people are dead inside, before their soul leaves their bodies". That happens when someone loses hope, I always sat alone and thought of people who are going through disabilities and some chronic illnesses, those people are the strongest and if you are about to lose hope I think you should look at them, no matter what disability they are facing, they always come up with a way to overcome it, they learned to accept the problem, and they came up with answers to conquer it and they are succeeding, I always looked at Oscar pistorius run, Natalie du tiot swim and masingita running her show on Soweto TV and asked myself why can't I learn from those who went through much than I did, It must have been hard for them, but they never looked back. Isn't it time for you to do the same?

YOU ARE A FIGHTER

For you to be born, you pushed yourself out of your mothers' womb and you didn't even give up because you had a purpose, that is why you fought to be out, why give up now when you are close to your destiny, when life gives lemons why don't you make lemonade? It tastes sour but one day you will enjoy it, they always say if you not enjoying and some are enjoying just don't worry because at the end life is cruel to all of us just not in the same day, while you in the darkness just hold on because one day it will be shining in your life. Remember you came as a warrior and survived many challenges and that is why you are here, look at military workers, they put their hope in God to safe their country so do the same and believe that with God all shall be well, fighters never quit because if they do, that will means they are failing themselves. Face your challenge and you will be okay. There is no mission that doesn't end. I always reminded myself that we will never achieve things the same ways, as we are all having our own disabilities. Some are good with numbers and some are good with words, etc. The little you lack is part of your disability, but even though it takes you time, if you don't give up you will one-day be ABLE. That's why you are here in the first place. You cried, crawled and started walking. What we both know is that even kids don't start walking on the same time, so that's achievement

Focus- as I said life is not about competing with the next party but with yourself, then you will get to realise that if you focus on your own mistakes or even failures. Nothing will get on your way, sometimes we get to focus on other people than we do on ourselves so sit down and evaluate yourself and mind your own business. You will see that life is not that bad, it only needed your attention.

Interactive- interacting with yourself and God through prayer is the best way to fight all. Let your inner voice and mind help you. It is never an answer to quit but then interacting with the inner you and telling yourself it will be alright. Believe, because nothing is impossible.

Guidance- guide yourself and turn to the right direction, if you get to see the causes of why you are in that situation that pushes you to take your life, please just at least change the direction and go to the right one, it is never late. Remember it's now or never. Be strong.

Hope- hope is the first step to achievement. If you can look at you and you alone and work hard, you will surely get to your destination. If you have a dream then follows it, that's your calling. If you want something to be true then you have all the reasons on earth to make that happen. Put hope against hope and stay strong.

Take over- we get to let other people to control us and tell us what to do that is really wrong. I think it is time to take the test and take over, and follow what you are meant to do not what people think is good for you. Take over your life because you deserve it.

TALKING COULD HELP

Talking has always had the power to oppose what the mind thinks, because when you start talking to someone or your paper, the pain get eased. What I would normally say is never ever and I will repeat that never place your deep secrets on social networks. I know you might think all of them care but no some don't even notice you exist. You have friends and a family you trust right? Go talk to them and let them know what's ringing in your mind. People who are mainly thinking of suicide always like acting strong and trying to show that they are happy but then that's not the solution. Showing how you feel is the key, I know you don't have to take it out on people and insult everyone you see, but then at least talk to someone, if you think what you are going through is not something you want your parents, family and your friends that's fine. Go see a professional and they will give you the solution. I strongly believe that everything don't just happen but there are steps, that is why in chemistry we have procedures in the practical laboratory and other forms of studies. I sometimes get to meet people in a public transport, sometimes I get to sit next to a person with problems, what they do is that they tell you everything they went through and even ask you what you think they must do and after advising them, they get relieved. Those kind of people are telling their problems because they know they don't know you and there is a slit chance of you two meeting again, even on Facebook someone just adds you and inboxes all her problems, after helping them, they block you. My remedy has always been my paper and a pen, I write what is bothering me, and I burn the paper after, I do this because I trust my God and my paper, I know this two will always have my back when I need help. After writing I just feel okay and the solutions just start coming into my head and all the negativity go away. I know it might sound crazy but then we all use different ways to get to the best solution.

TEARS! THE DILUTOR

Water has always helped in diluting a lot, now I think it's time you use that to your advantage, for Christ sake your tears do function in a lot of things but you can add something to what we already know, by just using them when you are down. I want to tell you that crying is the best remedy for pain. And if you feel like crying, then cry.

When a child is born and the first thing that welcomes him to earth is tears, because he is exposed to the world and ready to face it. There are tears of joy, sadness and maybe success. It is something that relieves a person and bring peace in his life, It really irritates me too that I cry a lot and I have made peace with it because it helps me in many ways, after my tears drip down I feel free and easy to forgive those who hurt me and forget what is haunting me. It gives my mind peace too.

It is one of the biggest gifts that God has made and people don't realise it, when someone cries they believe he is looking for attention or what's so ever, while the person is trying to make peace with what happened. Lord knows when I am alone I cry and all but then after that I feel free to move on with my life, I am a curious person who gets hurt easy and who wishes things can go my way. It is impossible I know. God seems to be a person who takes time to reply our request and really hurts some of us but as I said tears are there to comfort us and help us be patient. There are some things that you can't share with no one, not even a friend or you mom knows them, they just need you alone. If only we knew what is going to happen tomorrow hmm then I am telling you maybe things would be much better because we get curious and ask ourselves what tomorrow holds for us.

See you are not the only one facing hardship. We all do, no one promised that life was going to be simple but God promised to protect you no matter what. Why can't you cry to him and let him know whenever you are down. I mean pray!

I unpacked the word tears, into something positive, and I am hoping it will help you.

- **Test-** We are all tested, and when you are tested what has to be expected is if you will pass or fail that challenge. You have to study the problem and try to see what to do to trickle the challenge. Life is about challenges and without challenges we won't learn.
- **Experience-** the challenge is just an experience that needs your attention, and that just need you to be patient and be ready to face. Challenges, problems or whatever you call them will always

be there, even the rich face them. I know most people think wealth reduces problems but it doesn't. We will all experience something and we all have different problems in different situations.

- **Action-** I really don't believe in giving up and all but I know maybe you tried all the solutions but you then became depressed and thought the only solution is suicide but then my friend there is always a way out. You can and always know you can. Just take action, talk to someone and seek help. Your loved ones still care all you have to do is have the faith that you can get out of that silly problem, life is a gift and not gold or any money can exchange for it. Darlings play your part and let God be the one to own that life but not you. I believe you will get over it, now I think you have to believe in yourself. It's time to take charge of your life and not giving it up.

- **Results-** after acting on your problems, you will obviously get the results. What I can say is that if you chose to take good actions, you will find that the help you have been seeking and if you chose a bad action, a heart-breaking one, we will find that you are buried six feet under and that means you are no longer going to be seen, that plate you used to eat in will be useless, that chair you used to sit on won't be warm anymore and life for your family and those close to you will be tragic, you will leave a big gap on many things in is world, think of those who still love you and stop being selfish. Think about it. Is it what you want? I think when you taking the actions you have to make sure you are striving for best results.

- **Share your story**- every bad story that turned into good news must be shared, you can help others who can't talk out there, you can be a role model to some who were trying to take foolish decisions. Life is about learning and teaching the others. Remember you almost took the decision to commit suicide because you thought you were the only one who is unfortunate but then only to find that when you went to see the social worker or psychologist, there were many people who wanted to see him. So I think it's time to return the favour and show others that it is possible and all will be well. I can, you can and they can. Remember I believe in you.

Hope turning the tears into something nice and productive helped or will help you but then remember you have to live life and respect it.

VICTIM OF BEING PLAYED?

It is the latest trend that we see young people take their lives for a boyfriend/girlfriend. It might sound harsh but it is seriously what is happening these days, people play with their lives and kill their selves, hurting those who love them just to get to those who never cared. They are feeling guilty for what happened but then they still having their lives even today, they are succeeding and moving on. Maybe you might think just because the love of your life doesn't care about you then it is the end of the road and it is just not like that anymore. Love is a beautiful thing and everyone needs love, maybe when you are holding that rope, you are blaming yourself and love and asking yourself, why me? why did I have feelings for him/her and why did he say he loved me, while he didn't?, yes maybe you are curious and maybe you are beating yourself around trying to understand the reason it failed because it was so perfect, let me be honest with you, don't blame love because love is always there the problem is the people who are in love, don't blame yourself if you did the right thing and if it is your fault, every person deserves a second chance, even if it is not with the person you claim you love. People get played every day, one night stands are even a trend in the world of today, old men get to sleep with young girls and girls get to sleep around for money while boys are always waiting to sleep around. Why kill yourself for someone else's sins? They cheat on you and you crucify yourself for them, Jesus was the first and has to be the last man who died for other peoples sins, if you think of other people more than yourself then, you still have a lot to learn. Life doesn't need a coward who doesn't want to face their problems, life requires valiant. And they always say a valiant never taste death, but once. This means in life you don't die before your death date, you shouldn't give up and be a fool who can't face challenges, but then face them as a warrior, be brave and smart.

Overcoming issues doesn't really need studies; it needs a top-notch sharp mind that is not easily broken.

Sometimes we get to hear people saying someone is strong minded right? Yes when speaking of a strong minded person, we are not talking of a genius or an intelligent person, but a person who can think out of the box and tell himself that he will get out of the mess.

ACTIVATE YOUR MIND

Your mind is ready and it is sharp all it needs is a back-up plan, be a strong person and tell yourself that you have an elastic heart, after being hurt and going through hell it will fall back to place. Your heart can sometimes weaken your mind, they can be antagonistic but if you can try to balance them you will see miracles. The heart activates the mind and the heart needs your mind to get strong too. They work hand in hand. Suicide was never an answer and will never be an answer. The power of the tongue and mind can change your life, let your tongue remind you that you will make it and let your CPU record that one day the storm will be over and you will get your life back, won't be easy but this things need persistence, patience and perseverance.

We are all going through a stormy situation at some point but the weather will eventually change someday, we have summer, autumn, winter and spring as our seasons, so does our lives, they go through different seasons, some are fruitful and some are not. But we have to learn how to survive through each season, always be ready to go through to the next one, still happy and strong.

I believe God always has my back, I give myself time to tell him how I feel, and how thankful I am that I could see the next day and write this book, I even tell him when I feel like he is no longer watching me, but again why must I be selfish? How many people are sharing this world? We so many that God sometimes just want to test us and see who has faith and who believes in him, he did promise us that he will always be by our sides and we will see his blessings but for him to be sure that we believe in him he will test us like Job in the bible.

THE STORY OF JOB

The devil told God that Job was a perfect and an upright servant because he had everything every man wants, so God placed Job in a test and took all his 10 children, seven thousand sheep, three thousand camels, five thousand yoke of oxen and five hundred she asses and his great household, Job didn't complain he just fell on the ground and said, Naked came I out of my mother's womb, and naked shall I return thither: the Lord gave, and the Lord hath taken away; blessed be the name of the LORD. The devil was still not satisfied he told God that, the punishment was harsh but wasn't enough but God kept on saying 'has thou considered my servant Job, that there is none like him in the earth, a perfect and an upright man, one that feared God' but the devil answered God by saying skin for skin, Job was now sick, his skin was in pain and everyone could see that he was somehow covered by the cloud of curse. People came and comforted him but Job told them, this was meant to be, why did I not die from the womb? Why did I not give up the ghost when I came out of the belly? Why did the knees prevent me? Or why did I suck the breast? If I wasn't meant to be here and see this. –Job chapter 1-4

We could all see that Job's faith in God was strong, and he believed everything happened for a reason, he didn't kill himself or insult GOD, he believed that whatever that God gave him, he can still take it and he has his own reasons, I know it is hard but why not try to be like job?, why don't we let his will be done because he is the one who can give and take, job lost everything, maybe you lost a husband, a wife, a mother, father or a boyfriend dumped you and what came in your mind was suicide? Imagine if you lost everyone and everything you had, at least in your situation God is taking one and bringing something again, with job he made the test so difficult but he still believed that God knows what he doesn't know and that whatever he is going through is not a curse because he pushed himself out of the womb and that was for a cause. So be strong and keep telling daddy all and believing in him, he knows what's best for you and he knows what's still going to come in the future, don't be discouraged. Be strong.

The time will come, once you have fought the toughest situations of your life, just keep on living and you will see the miracle of life, things always get better with time and you will be alright. Believe in yourself and trust yourself. I know after a bad situation what I know is you will be in a healing process, because you were somehow spiritually crippled, you will start by crawling, then stand up and still fall a bit, then you will walk and will run. That's when you will be fine. Don't put pressure on yourself and learn that you are here for a purpose. We still need your kids to keep the generations going and I do care about you, so do the same, we never met but I am willing to give you a benefit of doubt. So it is time to look at yourself in a good way, because most out there care enough for you and pray for you each and every day.

CHAPTER 8

L.O.V.E

"There is no love or relationship that is right" – Thekgo

In life we all have the same characters but it is just that some are recessive on others and some are dominant, that is not impossible to make the bad ones recessive, for example when it comes to love some people make love to be dominant while some make it recessive. It takes time to make the right thing but it is always easy to do bad, know why? That is because love is rare. I always see people judge other people, when they see someone poor they say God is punishing them and when they see someone rich they say that person is illuminate, I know we all judge but ASAP Rocky in the song phoenix said a good statement that he never judge because Jesus never lied but was still crucified, which is true.

<u>SELF-LOVE</u>

What is love? This is a question that most people ask themselves, that is because it comes in different ways, greeting people is love, helping people is love, respecting people is love, etc.

Love is just like being tender-hearted, meaning you are easily moved to love, pity or sorrows. I always say first love yourself and you will know what love is, I sometimes get to see people who are confident and all that but the surprising part comes when the person starts pulling others down by hurting them with words and enjoying seeing others sad, that's where the confusion comes because that person has not accepted him/herself, meaning it is pretention because they are enjoying to see others sad and doubting themselves, maybe they want them to join the league of poor self-love.

Where the problem comes in? it mostly comes when you start imagining your life in someone else' life, trying to imitate Beyoncé or Nicki Minaj that is a problem, let Nicki Minaj be your role model maybe grasp the good side of her and you will be good, but trying to be her and even wanting to take her place then that is wrong, what's not wrong is if you learn the good from others, that is why we have mentors and all that.

> "If you are imagining your life in someone else's life then you have a problem because we all have our own purposes". – Thekgo

OPEN THE GIFT

I always tell my family that each and everyday things are getting better, the more you get to sleep and wake up the more things are happening, as I said on the previous chapter that we all here for a reason and God can't just create you to make you suffer. We all have a calling on earth that is why I discourage people to imitate and trying to see themselves in other peoples' lives. We all have a telepathic connection with God and our inner perfection, which is why we find our guts sometimes telling us things we never thought about, that's a gift to show that we all have a calling, some people are prophets, best surgeons, best teachers and etc. they found their calling that is why they succeed. I used to blame myself why I don't have a good voice, but then when I was growing up I had to Iearn about the gift of life and all. I personally just found myself interested in writing and falling in love with it, that was me unwrapping the gift, because when I am alone and bored the first thing I thought about was writing, and sometimes when I am busy my mind just thinks of a piece and then I write it and that gave me the interests in other peoples books, like David Molapo, John.C Maxwell, John Tibane, etc. That is why I am saying it's a calling. Maybe you know whenever you holding something electronic that is damaged; you can fix it without a manual that will assist you, some people change their career path after a long struggle in the higher institution because when they got to the work place, they get to realise that whatever they were doing is not for them. I know opening the gift or getting to reach your calling is not easy but I am going to assure you that it is going to happen and you will reach the goal. Sometimes we get to see our loved ones die and leaving us alone, dear if God thinks you have done what he brought you here for then he will come take you because he never promised us that we will be alive forever, he brought us naked and we are going back naked showing us that properties are nothing but what's important is accomplishing the mission, there is endless life after death so why stress because when you are done he will tell you to come back home were you will suffer no more. Focus on you and not the other person, some people say that between the date of birth and date of death there is a dash, and that dash is your obituary, telling the nation what you have done, that is where exposure to your calling will be in public, so be careful and do what God brought you here for, learn to leave the world with peoples' hearts filled with love and joy.

SHOWING SOME LOVE

"Love shouldn't be self-infatuated but
self-abandoned" – Thekgo

My grandfather used to work at a farm and every Wednesday, he would ask his boss to release him so that he can go to church, the boss never stopped him from going but one day he decided not to release him, then my grandfather told him that he must thank God that he is happy, healthy and still surviving and wanted to pray for blessing meaning he wanted the boss to release him but then the boss looked at him and said "Joe you are selfish, is that why you go to church every day?, if so then I don't regret staying here and taking care of the farm, I thought you were going to church to learn how to love". While my grandfather was still surprised and out of words, the boss took his truck and told him to jump in and as he wanted to show him something, they then took a ride and they went to a nearby 4way stop, and many people were standing next to the pedestrian line trying to cross the road because the cars were running, what the boss did was that he stopped and the people could cross the road, while they were passing they waved to him and saying thank you, he then told my grandfather that in life if you want blessings from God try to make his people happy and when they say thank you that is a blessing, he then told him look at the blessings you gained today, just by showing love. When my father shared the story his father told him, I learned that love helps us gain blessings.

RELATIONSHIPS

We are all related to someone that is why we have to keep the love burning because that will bring us peace and a good relationship. The connection must come from the inner, people won't get to feel neglected around you and that's where the relationship starts. If you can look at the word relationship, it was built from two words which is relation and a ship, we all know a relation is some sort of connection but let's look more on the word ship, this ship is like a ship in the sea or the ocean, it puts you in a test of life, with the people you with in that ship, it can be a friendship, companionship, etc.

They don't end with a ship for nothing, in life we get to choose those we want in our lives and those we want to share it with, but most importantly even if some are not in the ship with you maybe just try to accommodate them by trying to smile at them and greet them, and stop with the hating and fighting, every relationship has a beginning.

LET'S LOOK AT THE WORD "SHIP"

SHARING- To give and to receive is a good way to explain sharing, in a ship selfishness is not needed; you have to work together and believe in one another. Don't undermine the other one but at least try to help him by correcting the mistake, in this ship you need to look beyond your eyesight. See what the future will be if you pass this ocean to a new world of sharing, it start by sharing a smile, a laugh, a blanket, the problems and the good times. If you can share that I am pretty sure, you can share whatever that comes your way. No need to prove that you are a good driver or maybe a good sailor, if you good teach your partner because no competing is needed; it is a teaching and learning moment. Learn to ask for forgiveness and also forgive.

HOPE- hope goes hand in hand with trust, when you get in the middle of the ocean faraway from where you from, it is going to be a bit tough, that's were problems arise, maybe you starting to judge each other, starting to compare, starting to undermine and maybe getting to know their weakness which may become unattractive to you, or maybe you are starting to doubt yourself around the person. But with trust and hope that you will make it to the other side and even if you are forced to go back you can get there safely then consider it done.

INTEREST- if you are interested in something all your attention will go to that thing, on 'H' I told you that it will be a bit bumpy because true colours and weaknesses are arising, but if you want to stick to your partner and your partner also wants to stick to you then you will try to solve all your problems and come with the solution, that's were your input is important, accepting when you are wrong and saying when something is bothering you, if you are interested you will communicate and will solve whatever that happened, I always heard people saying we must stop blaming love, and start blaming the people, love has always been there but the problem came when people started hating, discriminating and judging.

PARTNERSHIP- if you are a partner with someone, there must be something that connected you with that certain person; it can be business, love, trust or maybe friendship. You have joined your imperfections to be perfect. We get to see some people who can't work without their assistance and are surprised; those two are somehow connected, if the other one is not around the other can't operate. So even you in that ship you must learn to work hand in hand with your partner, consider them in your decisions and let them help you were you are lacking, it fun! Try it!

CHAPTER 9

DEATH

"Death is a normal process of life, we just
have to learn to get used to It" – Thekgo

I am sure that you are asking yourself, why did I take my time to write about death, well I have realised the subject scares us to an extend that seeing this five letters freaks us out, while the truth is we should not live in worry but celebrate life instead. I know to some it is a taboo, but sometimes we just have to be open about it, talking to the little ones and so forth, it is not to scary them but to teach them that dying is not a way of God to punish us, but it's his way of creating angels we had the chance to interact with us, as the person next to you that is no longer with us will always live in you.

We are all waiting in suspense, regardless of our race, age, religion, time or state with no idea of when we are going to die as I said in the beginning that life is unpredictable but are you certain that you have served your part at this moment?, cause I believe God takes those who have played their role, my easy example is Nelson Rolihlahla Mandela, he was in prison for 27 years and he survived, that made me realize that he didn't die because he was intelligent or maybe perfect but his purpose on earth was not done, he was the chosen one from birth to reconcile the whites and the blacks in south Africa, to cease apartheid and bring peace.

We do mistakes and we do foolish things but at the end of the day we learn from them, life is not about perfection, it is about learning from the imperfect of others. When someone is dead we always hear many stories about how early that person left us or how good-hearted s/he was but at the end of the day we have to accept that nature took its part, it was never our decision to make and will never be. It is sad when you lose the one close to you when you still need them most, yes it is unfair when something like that happens but let me remind you, the road you are going to walk on is yours alone and if it is the end of someone's road you don't have to be discouraged, at least try to accept that it is over but you still have your part to play too because you are powerless to prevent or overcome death, all we praying for is to at least get to our grave as winners not failures.

WHY ARE FUNERALS DIGNIFIED?

Saying your last goodbye is the saddest moment a person can wish for, if you want to know that life is funny, you will get to realise that even if you believed you hated someone, once they announce that the person is no more, you will always have that soft spot and maybe blame yourself sometimes because you never gave yourself time to know the person but to fight them and hate them for many things, it even gets funnier when one of the worst criminal is getting the biggest last respect, well I did my research and found that all the evil and the good are done by the soul, so now that the soul left the innocent body then the body deserves respect because it was just the carrier of that person. It is confusing but makes sense, when the soul leaves the body, you will see that the body is helpless and so innocent, you can even see peace in it. So let us not blame it because it is somehow not bad.

"Before death we get to learn that in life we have to be ready for death, even if we are left in suspense, we are eager to know what is going to happen and how, so that we can show love and appreciation to life before it is too late" – Thekgo

STORY OF LIFE

Read this piece maybe you will learn something like I did when I first saw it, I don't know the writer but it gives us a lead.

Apparently we all have four wives in our lives, lean more…

- The fourth wife is our body. The one we surely love so much and the one we use to show off, go everywhere with and the one we respect the most but when we are sick and in pain and about to die, it runs away from us and doesn't care about us anymore.
- The third wife is our work position, power in the community and all the luxury and fame, we also love the 3rd wife too, but when we are in pain and sick on the hospital bed, the 3rd wife will surely replace you because you are about to die, remember it doesn't care at all, all it does is use you to forget who you are.
- The second wife is our family and friends and those people close to us, they will always be there for you, through every bad or good thing in our lives but when you sick and about to die there is nothing they can do, the least they can offer is to be beside your bed and be ready to say goodbye because you are leaving alone this time. They might have been with you through everything but this time they won't and really can't help you.
- The first is the SOUL, the one you never give your attention, the one you hated, the one you undermined, the one you excluded and never gave your all to, were ever you are or still going surely it will follow you. Even on your hospital bed when

you are helpless and out of ideas, looking at your grave, always know it will face death with you and will it will never fail you like the three other wives. So at least look after her because she will always be the real wife amongst them.

THE SOUL

"Many thought that glitters and fame would bring them happiness, but forgetting that if the soul is not monitored well then, nothing will be interesting despite the fact that they have it all" – Thekgo

The soul is an important component of life as in reality it is the only "real self", our physical covering is just temporary. We can trade our organs but we can never trade our soul to the next person, you can change your outer beauty but you can never change the real you, because that is our essence.

"For what will it profit a man if he gains the whole world, and loses his own soul? Or what will a man give in exchange for his soul?" – Mk 8:36-7

That was Jesus' words to his disciples, and in them we get to learn that the soul is more valuable and that we may have all the wealth but no one can afford the price of the soul, if you can just take your time and read the story of Lazarus and the rich man you will get to learn about the importance of your soul, the scripture helps us understand that once we cross over to death, which is the eternal life. There are no more chances. Our eternal state takes place at the moment we die.

The soul is important because a man was created in the image of God so if you do badly you are reflecting God in a bad way, as God doesn't have a physical body like ours that just simply mean God has to be seen through our spirit and soul. What you must circumspectly be aware of is that our physique is made of genes and we can change that with plastic surgeries and fitness training but that will never stop the process of dying and getting old, but with soul you can try to change it by giving thanks to the lord and changing that negative attitude. We get to learn that even if we can avoid God now and do as we want but it won't last, because when we die our bodies will return to dust and our souls and spirits are going back to the creator.

WHAT DO WE TRADE OUR SOULS FOR?

Trading is like a business transition, whereby we get to buy shares with lots of money to be in the cooperate world, but that is not what I want to tell you about, I know we all love the lavish lifestyle and nobody want to be poor but sometimes I think most of us are just overdoing it by going extreme to be rich and famous and forget our services to the Lord, I mean forgetting your purpose is just now going out of hand. There is a nice poem I once read trying to show us if we can all be educated and avoid the dirty jobs but how will the world be? Imagine if there were no people who pick up our dirty dustbins every morning, all those who wash our laundry when we are in our offices and those who cut your lawn and clean the toilet you messed up, they are many and when you rich and above them you start to undermine them, do you think that's fair? Yes you may be good at your job because God chose you to do that but why don't you appreciate other people's calling? At least understand other peoples' situation because your life is not guaranteed that it will be perfect forever, you can lose your hands in an accident and get a replacement in your office and that will be a lesson from God that your life is in the palm of his hand. We should understand we are not the same because in everything balance is needed. For some I can't defend them because they just trade their soul through laziness, which is the worst because it is like you are dead but still walking and waking up every day. It hurts when people just decide to sit and do nothing; I believe it's a sin to be relaxed because we are here to plant our future and harvest in a later stage even on our death bed.

If you don't save your own soul regardless of your wealth state and position in life you are a complete failure, you may have a million friends and all the money that can buy all luxury that will mourn your death, but if the soul is still nothing to you that will be a total disgrace, you must even keep in mind even if you are poor and not in a good state if your soul is saved that will be a successful depart because your life was marvellous.

<u>DO WE HAVE TO FEAR DEATH?</u>

No! I am saying no because I know every day when we live we are learning to die, everything is dangerous, even drinking water is not safe cause you can drink water and enter the wrong pipe and die.

Doctors can say to me, lying in the coffin, "she had a heart failure, couldn't survive death or got an accident", but that is nothing because the day I die, I am the engine of my body, my body is just a suit so that I can live on earth, it has no life that's when the real me will leave it as an empty suit. As we know we are visitors here even though some visit longer than some, I want us to all look at death in a positive eye, because we don't really die but just going back home were we belong. We have to give each other a chance when someone dies, someone is born and that is just the circle of life.

I know the fear of death comes when we start seeing the death of the young ones and the killings happening every day, but I believe God really wants us to live longer and have a full life. Remember the story of job I wrote for you? God's will is done, because he knows the days you have to live and be satisfied.

"He shall call upon me, and I will answer him:
I will be with him in trouble; I will deliver him,
and honour him. With long life I will satisfy him,
and show him my salvation." – Psalm 91:15-16

We have to understand that to God death is just a departure, it like leaving earth and going to join him, which I think is better.

I personally wish that people don't weep when I am gone, because after my death I am going to be in peace, even if it can hurt a few they must at least do me a favour by moving on and making everyday a normal day as my memories will live when I am gone, if God takes me then it is time because I have overcame the things I never thought I will so why should I fear death? You don't have to lie down in bed afraid that you might not wake up, because death has no timing, it can happen anytime if that's the time.

"Death is like facing your opponent in a boxing match, if you face him with some trepidation, he will surely knock you out, but if you can get in the ring unconcern, the chances are least because he will be intimidated by your confidence" – Thekgo

WHAT DEATH TEACHES US?

It teaches us to understand the joy of life and will teach you how important life is and why we must enjoy every second we live here, we connect, bond and share love, the nurturing, and the memories. All that are the gift of life and death get to remind us to hold on to them, because we know they won't last. As I said even if your enemy dies you will realise you had a soft spot for that person that you didn't know, so at least learn to love because love is transcendent, with no termination and reaches yonder in the physicality of life.

There more we lose our loved ones we realise that life is not permanent and that nothing last forever no matter how much you try to protect it. We also learn to accept that life is about moving forward and if you don't accept death you will never move forward.

Death is the one that points to us what being alive is and what it means. When you have a purpose, you are guided internally, telepathically so. You are connecting beyond what you thought you are. Death humble us and takes us to the possibility of waking up and making a change, were we get to do what's really important. What we must learn is that never wait for someone to die so that you can change the way you live.

We view life as a gift, meaning death is just were life stops and coming to an end. But it is also entering a new beginning.

We must remember that life is precious and fragile, learn to enjoy the small things in life and stop with that daily routine, get to see the world and explore, stop with the hunger for materialistic things and spend quality time with your friends and family. Reduce the complaining and enjoy life, be grateful for what God has given you and focus on having a big heart by trying to lead a good life where you will enjoy quality moments with your closed ones and spread happiness and love around you.

CONCLUDING REMARKS

"We meet each other for different purposes; we meet some for a lesson, some for an experiment and some to teach what we learned, so it is good to acknowledge anything that comes your way, because you are what you are today because of that" – Thekgo

We are in a new world of purposes, fights are few and we are somehow moving forward, it is really time to realise we all go through bumpy ways but we will overcome them. I am trying to make you see life in another angle and learn to accept what comes your way, patience and know that we are here for a purpose and all will be okay, we are a generation that can change the way the world is and for that to happen is if we stick together. Life shouldn't be something hard, let's evolve the image now before the next century, for the world to be a better place.

We can make it and I believe we will. The little that our elders did is something, why can't we leave our own foot print.

To be able to understand the future we must understand the past, I hope I have tried to share the past now we know what we can do to evolve what we are today, we have to make a change.

"History is not just there to teach you about where you are from, but to open your eyes that there is more to it that you can learn, so that you can pave the future, because without it there is no future" – Thekgo

We are trying to change the future because we have seen that even though it is better now we can keep practicing to make it much better. We are now still picturing the future looking at the current situation so that we can pass it on the next generation, the decisions we make today will surely result in the future. Hopefully HIV/Aids and most chronic diseases will be curable, and we will maybe have few poor people and to win that we have to respect and love one another not based on race or religion but because we are human. We must stop being egocentric and trying to show others we are the best because in this world we are all connected on the cycle of life then that way our kids will learn to live in peace and love no matter what.

I hope we are in this together and we
will surely get good results

LAW OF ATTRACTION

The law of attraction states that every positive or negative event that happened with you was attracted by you. Which means if we can positively look at the current situation so that our results can come out positive too, we are now creating thoughts to the universe and the universe will surely give us the answers we need, we have to be sure of what we want and the results will come as we wish. That is why we need each other and believe in our thoughts that will change the future. They always say that the ones that think of failure will have failure and those who think of prosperity have prosper. I am in a mission of attracting a better future too. According to the book 'when you think a little thought of something that we want, through the law of attraction, that thought grows larger and greater" so it is time to look at the changes we want as we hope they should be, not as they are. Let's not worry about what our dreams are but use them to guide us.

REFERENCES

Introduction
Source: http://www.jr.co.il/articles/women.txt

Chapter 1
Dr David Molapo, 2011, choose to change, South Africa, struik Christian books

Chapter 2
Source: www.teachballroomdancing.com/2014/10/the-program-has-made-a-real-and-positive-impact-in-my-life/

Chapter 4
Source: www.askmen.com/dating/players

Chapter 5
Source: www.lfcc.on.ca/HCT_SWASM_4.html

Chapter 6
Source: www.msureschco.com/about6.htm

Source: www.dailymail.co.uk/news/article-2123757/girls-lack-confidence-appearance-blighting-futures.html
Source: http://tinybuddha.com/blog/the-secret-to-instant-self-confidence/

Chapter 7
Source: https://imwiththeclouds.tumblr.com/post/38347319557/100-reasons-to-why-you-shouldnt-commit-suicide

Chapter 9
Deepak Chopra, 2004, the book of secrets: unlocking the hidden dimensions of your life, three rivers press
Source: https://bible.org/seriespage/lesson-50-trading-your-soul-what-genesis-2527-34-heb-1216-17
Source: http://loveinfinitely.org/what-death-teaches-us/
Source: https://executableoutline.com/matt/mt16_26.htm

About the Author

In need of guidance and support from someone who understands? In A Young Woman Evolving the Vision of the Future, a twenty-year-old and brand-new motivational speaker, Thekgo Nkadimeng, is trying to teach you how to overcome all the hardships in your life. She believes in support and hard work.

Printed in the United States
By Bookmasters